my first book of questions and answers

long ago

Maggie Brown

p

This is a Parragon Publishing Book
First published in 2002

Parragon Publishing
Queen Street House
4 Queen Street
Bath BA1 1HE, UK

Produced by

David West 🏃 Children's Books
7 Princeton Court
55 Felsham Road
Putney
London SW15 1AZ, UK

British Library Cataloguing-in-Publication Data

A catalogue record for this book is available from
the British Library.

Hardback ISBN 0-75257-579-1
Paperback ISBN 0-75257-708-5

Printed in China

Designers
Aarti Parmar, Rob Shone, Fiona Thorne

Illustrators
Gerry Haylock, Andy Lloyd Jones, Pete Roberts
(Allied Artists)

Cartoonist
Peter Wilks (SGA)

Editor
James Pickering

CONTENTS

4 When was the age of exploration?

4 When did Columbus reach the Americas?

5 Who first sailed around the world?

6 Where was the New World?

7 Who sailed in the Mayflower?

7 Was Pocahontas a real person?

8 Who were the sea dogs?

9 Who was the scariest pirate?

10 What was the slave trade?

10 Who was Queen Nzingha?

11 Who said "Dr Livingstone, I presume?"

12 Who sailed in the Endeavour?

13 Which explorers died in the outback?

14 How many wives did Henry VIII have?

15 Who was good Queen Bess?

15 What was the Armada?

16 Who painted the world's most famous painting?

16 Which great artist painted a ceiling?

17 Who wrote Romeo and Juliet?

18 Where is the world's most beautiful tomb?

18 Who lived in the Forbidden City?

19 Why was Ivan terrible?

20 Who was the Sun King?

21 Which English king lost his head?

22 Which French king lost his head?

23 Who crowned himself emperor of France?

23 When was the Battle of Waterloo?

24 When was the American Revolution?

24 Who was the first US president?

25 What was the Boston Tea Party?

26 When did Americans head west?

26 Why did Americans fight a civil war?

27 Who won the Battle of Little Big Horn?

28 Who was the lady with the lamp?

28 When was the Victorian age?

29 When did women win the vote?

30 What was the Industrial Revolution?

31 Why did the 20th century get off to a flying start?

32 Index

When was the age of exploration?

The great age of European exploration began in the 1400s, as sailors hunted for sea routes to the Indies – India, China, Japan and Indonesia. Back then, spices and silks were exotic goods that were only found in the Indies. They were worth a fortune, but overland travel was very slow. A sea route would be quicker – if it could be found.

Europe

Indies

When did Columbus reach the Americas?

The Viking journeys to North America were long forgotten when Christopher Columbus headed west from Spain across the Atlantic Ocean in August 1492. Two months later, on October 12th, he landed on an island in the Caribbean Sea.

Christopher Columbus

? *Who first sailed around the world?*

In September 1519, five ships set off from Spain under the command of Ferdinand Magellan. Although Magellan died during the voyage, and only one ship made it home in 1522, his expedition was the first to sail right around the world.

Ferdinand Magellan

Where was the New World?

Before Columbus stumbled across the Americas, Europeans thought the world was made up of Europe, Africa and Asia. Europeans called the Americas the New World. Nations such as Spain, France and England began to establish colonies – settlements abroad, ruled by the settlers' home country.

Pilgrims

?Who sailed in the Mayflower?

The Mayflower was the ship that carried a group of 102 English settlers to the east coast of North America in 1620. The settlers, who became known as the Pilgrims, founded a colony there.

Mayflower

?Was Pocahontas a real person?

She certainly was – Pocahontas was a Native American. An English settler called John Smith claimed that she saved his life when she was a girl. In 1614, Pocahontas married another settler, John Rolfe.

Pocahontas

Francis
Drake

Blackbeard

?Who were the sea dogs?

By the 1550s, Spanish ships were carrying gold and other treasure from their American colonies back to Spain. The sea dogs were English captains like Francis Drake who raided the Spanish treasure ships. They were under secret orders from their queen, Elizabeth I.

Who was the scariest pirate?

The most terrifying pirate of all time was Blackbeard (whose real name was Edward Teach). To make him look extra-fierce in battle, he wove ropes through his hair and lit them – many of his victims were so scared they gave up without a fight! Despite his fierce reputation, Blackbeard was a pirate for only a few years before he was captured and killed in 1718.

What was the slave trade?

During the 1500s, Europeans began a cruel trade in slaves – people with no rights, who are completely owned by their master. Traders took African men, women and children from their homelands to suffer lives of great hardship, working as slaves in the American colonies.

Slave trading

Who was Queen Nzingha?

Nzingha was an African warrior queen, who fought to stop Europeans invading her lands in western Africa and taking her people for the slave trade. She was 81 when she died in 1663.

Queen Nzingha

Who said "Dr Livingstone, I presume?"

Livingstone and Stanley

These were newspaper reporter Henry Stanley's first words when he met explorer Dr David Livingstone in Central Africa in 1871. Although Europeans had explored the African coastline by the late 18th century, none had traveled into the continent's heart. Livingstone was the first European to travel across Africa, in 1853–56.

Endeavour

Who sailed in the Endeavour?

In 1768, Captain James Cook left England in the Endeavour, heading for the Pacific Ocean. Two years later, he became the first European to set foot on Australia's east coast.

? *Which explorers died in the outback?*

In 1860, a large cash prize was offered to the first settlers to cross the Australian continent. Robert Burke and William Wills became the first to do this, traveling from south to north in 1861. Sadly, the pair never reached home again – they died of starvation in the outback on their return journey.

Burke and Wills

Catherine Parr   Jane Seymour   Anne of Cleves   Henry VIII   Catherine of Aragon   Anne Boleyn   Catherine Howard

❓How many wives did Henry VIII have?

Henry VIII of England is famous for chopping and changing his wives. He had six in all – two were beheaded, two were divorced, and one died having a baby. Luckily for the last one, they were still married when Henry died in 1547.

Who was good Queen Bess?

This was one of the nicknames of Henry VIII's daughter, Elizabeth I, who ruled England from 1558 to 1603. Her reign is often called the golden age because it was a time of great writers such as William Shakespeare, and bold sea captains such as Walter Raleigh and Francis Drake.

Queen Elizabeth I

Spanish Armada

What was the Armada?

The Armada was a fleet of 130 ships sent by King Philip II of Spain to invade England in 1588. It was a disaster for the Spanish. Their ships were driven away, and nearly half sank in storms.

Who painted the world's most famous painting?

Leonardo and the Mona Lisa

The world's most famous painting is the Mona Lisa, and it was created in the early 1500s by one of the greatest artists of all time, Leonardo da Vinci.

Michelangelo painting the Sistine Chapel

Which great artist painted a ceiling?

The Italian Michelangelo was another artistic genius of the 1500s. One of his greatest works was the ceiling of the Sistine Chapel in the Vatican, in Rome, which showed the history of the world according to the Bible.

❓ Who wrote Romeo and Juliet?

The love story of Romeo and Juliet was written by perhaps the greatest playwright of all time, Englishman William Shakespeare. The play was first performed in the 1590s.

William
Shakespeare

Shakespeare's
Globe Theater

❓ Where is the world's most beautiful tomb?

The Taj Mahal in India was built by the Emperor Shah Jahan as a tomb for his beloved wife, Mumtaz Mahal, who died in 1629. It is made from gleaming white marble and surrounded by a beautiful garden.

Taj Mahal

❓ Who lived in the Forbidden City?

The Ming emperors ruled China from 1368 to 1644. Their beautiful palaces in the city of Beijing were in an area which was called the Forbidden City, because ordinary people weren't allowed to enter.

Forbidden City

Why was Ivan terrible?

Ivan IV of Russia was nicknamed the Terrible because he was such a brutal ruler – anyone who opposed him was killed. Ivan wasn't all bad, though. He made Russia into a strong country, and in 1547 he became the first Russian ruler to be crowned czar.

Ivan the Terrible

Louis XIV

?*Who was the Sun King?*

Louis XIV of France was the most magnificent European ruler of the 1600s. He was called the Sun King because of his glitteringly luxurious lifestyle, and he once acted the part of the Sun in a splendid ballet at his palace of Versailles, near Paris. Like other kings of his day, Louis believed that his right to rule was given to him by God, and that parliamentary rule by the people was wrong.

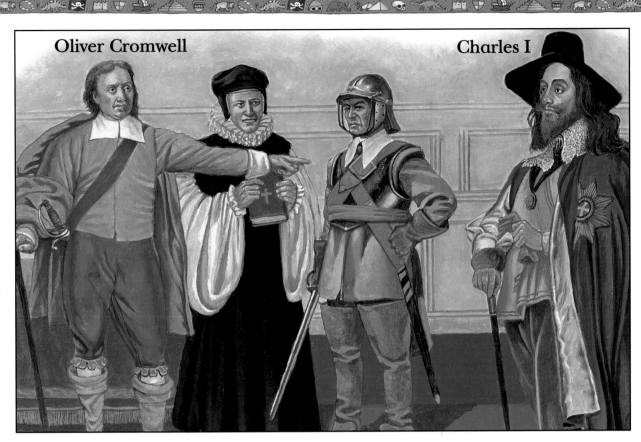

Oliver Cromwell

Charles I

❓ Which English king lost his head?

Charles I's head was chopped off in 1649, after his supporters, the Royalists, lost the civil war against the Parliamentarians led by Oliver Cromwell. Civil war had broken out in 1642, following Charles's attempts to rule the country without a parliament.

Louis XIV's courtiers watched him getting dressed.

TRUE. It was a great honor to be chosen to do this, and to be given a special job such as holding the king's coat.

Cromwell's supporters were called Roundheads.

TRUE. The name came from their short haircuts, which were the total opposite of the Royalists' style – long curls.

Which French king lost his head?

By 1789, the French people had had enough of their kings' extravagant lifestyles and arrogant ways of ruling. A revolution broke out, with the people rising up against King Louis XVI and his nobles. Four years later, Louis was beheaded on a machine called the guillotine.

Louis XVI

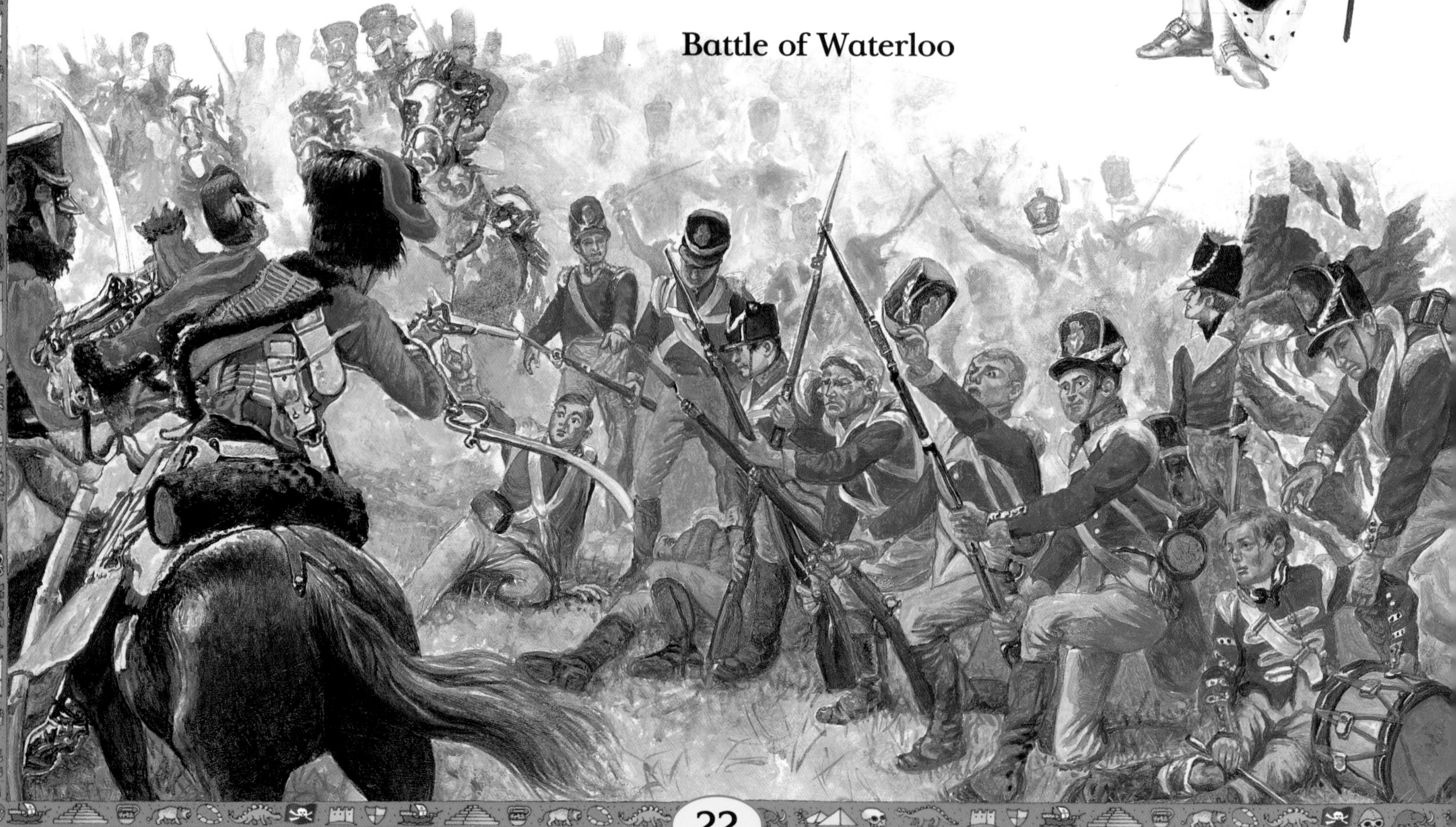

Battle of Waterloo

Who crowned himself emperor of France?

Napoleon

The French Revolution ended in 1799 when Napoleon Bonaparte took over the government. Napoleon was a brilliant ruler and general, who conquered a huge empire. In 1804, he crowned himself emperor in Paris, the French capital.

When was the Battle of Waterloo?

Waterloo took place in Belgium on June 18th, 1815 and was Napoleon's last battle. His power was smashed when his army was defeated by the British, led by the Duke of Wellington and the Prussians, led by Marshal Blücher.

When was the American Revolution?

By the 1750s, American settlers lived in 13 British colonies along the east coast. They had had enough of British rule and they were fed up with paying taxes to the British parliament, thousands of miles away across the Atlantic Ocean. War broke out between the Americans and the British in April 1775, and lasted for eight years.

George Washington

Who was the first US president?

In 1789, six years after Americans won their independence from Britain, George Washington became the first president of the US.

? *What was the Boston Tea Party?*

No one drank tea at the Boston Tea Party of 1773. Instead, fed up with paying the tax on tea, a group of colonists disguised themselves as Native Americans, crept on board some British ships, and threw their cargoes of tea into Boston Harbor.

Boston Tea Party

When did Americans head west?

At first, the United States was made up of lands east of the Mississippi River. The lands to the west were still French, Spanish and British colonies. In 1803 the United States began to buy these colonies, and settlers moved west.

Settlers heading west

Why did Americans fight a civil war?

Americans from the northern states wanted to end slavery. The southern states didn't, and a civil war broke out. In 1865, the northern states won and slavery was banned.

Northern soldiers

Little Big Horn

Who won the Battle of Little Big Horn?

At the Battle of Little Big Horn in 1876, Native American warriors defeated US General Custer and his army.

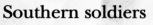

Southern soldiers

? Who was the lady with the lamp?

Nurse Florence Nightingale was. Hospitals were dirty, unhygienic places when Florence started nursing in the 1850s, and she spent her life fighting to improve health care and training.

Queen Victoria

Florence Nightingale

? When was the Victorian age?

The Victorian age was named after Queen Victoria, who ruled Britain from 1837 to 1901. Her reign of 63 years is the longest in British history.

When did women win the vote?

The women of Wyoming in the United States were the first to win the right to vote in local elections, in 1869. However, the women of New Zealand were the first to vote in national elections, in 1893.

Protesting for the right to vote

TRUE OR FALSE?

Queen Victoria never married.

FALSE. She married her cousin, Prince Albert, in 1840 and they had nine children.

Women couldn't be doctors in Victorian times.

FALSE. It was difficult, but a few did. The first American woman doctor was Elizabeth Blackwell, back in 1849.

What was the Industrial Revolution?

The Industrial Revolution began in the 1700s, with the invention of new steam-powered machines for making things. Factories were built, and towns grew up to house factory workers. Most goods were handmade before this time, and most ordinary people lived and worked in the country.

Wright brothers' first flight

❓ Why did the 20th century get off to a flying start?

The 1800s were a hugely inventive time, when scientists dreamed up many everyday things – from light bulbs to telephones (the 1870s), and steam trains (1804) to gas-driven cars (1885). The invention that got the 20th century off to a flying start was the powered aircraft – first flown by brothers Orville and Wilbur Wright in 1903.

Children worked in factories and mines during the 1700s.

TRUE. Children as young as four worked a 12-hour day. Governments passed laws banning this in the 1800s.

The first skyscrapers were built in the 1880s.

TRUE. Even buildings were heading for the sky!

Index

Armada, the 15

Blackbeard 9

Boston Tea Party 25

Burke, Robert 13

Charles I 21

Columbus, Christopher 4, 5

Cook, James 12, 13

Cromwell, Oliver 21

Custer, General 27

Drake, Francis 8, 15

Elizabeth I 8, 15, 19

Forbidden City 18

Henry VIII 14

Industrial Revolution 30

Ivan the Terrible 19

Leonardo da Vinci 16, 17

Little Big Horn, Battle of 27

Livingstone, David 11

Louis XIV 20, 21

Magellan, Ferdinand 5

Michelangelo 16

Napoleon 23

Nightingale, Florence 28

Nzingha, Queen 10

Pilgrims, the 7

Pocahontas 7

Shakespeare, William 15, 17

Stanley, Henry 11

Taj Mahal 18

Victoria, Queen 28

Washington, George 24

Waterloo 23

Wills, William 13

Wright brothers 31

Zheng He 19